D1155329

The Angel in Ebony

or

The Life and Message
of Sammy Morris

by

Jorge O. Masa

Published by
Class of 1928 of Taylor University

Taylor University Press
Upland, Indiana
USA

Taylor University Press, Upland, Indiana 46989

© 2004, by Taylor University Press
All rights reserved
First Edition published 1928
Second Edition 2004
Second Printing 2006
Printed in the United States of America

ISBN: 0-9740758-2-5

TABLE OF CONTENTS

SAMMY MORRIS
"The Angel In Ebony"

THE ANGEL IN EBONY

FOREWARD

What an amazing on-going phenomenon:
Samuel Kaboo Morris, a student from
Liberia who attended Taylor University in
the late 19th century and died of a respira-
tory illness after only 18 months, continues
to touch lives as one of the most significant
individuals who has influenced the institution since her beginnings in 1846.

Of several books written about Morris,
this volume is outstanding. Jorge O. Masa,
a brilliant Taylor student from the Philippines, wrote this account with an understanding of the racial insensitivity that
Morris may have felt at the time the story
occurred. He personally interviewed several
members of the Taylor University con-
stituency who had known Morris and had
intimate, extensive conversations with him.

Masa had come to Taylor University

full of doubt as to the validity of faith
in Christ as taught and witnessed to by
members of the community. Soon after
his arrival, he was given a copy of the first
book written about Morris. Although emo-
tionally touched by the story, he concluded
that the African's religious experiences
were "unreal, if not fanatical." Four years
later, as Masa neared the completion of
his studies, he re-read the booklet. This
time, the reality of the faith of this African student convinced his doubting mind
and he became a believer. In Masa's own
words, Samuel Morris taught him that "a
perfect surrender to the will and love of
God that is in Christ Jesus will bring about
a transformation of attitude, ideals, and of
life itself."

After graduation from Taylor in 1928,
Masa completed graduate studies at
Columbia and Yale Universities. Upon his
return to the Philippines he became an

outstanding church leader and performed a number of heroic feats in saving lives and encouraging believers during World War II.

How do we account for the amazing influence of Samuel Morris? How do we explain the fact that this unlettered young man, with no earthly credentials, came from "nowhere" to attend a struggling American university and was instrumental in saving it from bankruptcy or extinction? How do we explain the buildings, scholarships and other monuments established in his honor? How do we explain the inquiries that keep coming from around the world, telling stories like Masa's, of the way this account has changed their lives? Simply stated, we recognize this as testimony to the power of the Holy Spirit.

Dr. Charles B. Kirkpatrick
Professor Emeritus
Taylor University

DR. C. B. STEMEN

CAPE PALMAS, W. AFRICA
Where Sammy took ship

THE ANGEL IN EBONY

PREFACE

I was struggling to find for myself a perfectly satisfying interpretation of life. I had come to a point where doubt had taken hold of my mind; I could not seem to see the optimism in Christian faith. The seeming contradictions that were apparent in many aspects of human life nearly drove me to despair and pessimism. But on the other hand, my honest soul was dissatisfied, and would not rest until it discovered the something truly certain. Does life have a meaning? Is God in Jesus Christ reconciling the world unto Himself? These questions faced me, and silently I groped to find an answer for them.

It was four years ago when the life of Sammy Morris was given me by a kind friend. I read the brief little sketch at about eleven o'clock at night, when all was solemn and quiet. My eyes were moist as I turned the pages of that thrilling spiritual adventure, so uncommon in the twentieth century. But I could not understand it. I went to bed with a proud justification in my mind that Sammy's religious experiences were unreal, if not fanatical. I did not know Jesus then.

Last year I opened once more the little pamphlet and started to interpret the meaning of Sammy Morris's religious experiences. I had just read Begbie's "Twice Born Men," and Professor James's "Varieties of Religious Experiences." A question struck me: Is there a reality in the faith of the poor African boy -- a reality to help convince my doubting mind of the truths in the Christian religion? I found that there is. Sammy Morris, the uncultured, uncouth African boy, taught me that a perfect surrender to the will and love of God that is in Christ Jesus will bring about the transformation of attitude, ideals, and of life itself. Here was reality. I tried it, and it worked.

THE ANGEL IN EBONY

Since then I conceived the idea of writing a more extended biography of the Kroo boy so that people might see this beautiful instance of the redeeming power of the Christian religion. When the Gift Committee of the 1928 Senior Class visited Fort Wayne to study the possibilities of perpetuating the memory of Sammy Morris, it was suggested by one member that I undertake the task of rewriting his biography. It was a joy, but it meant responsibility. I wondered how I could do it.

In the first place, I had little time to spare to perform so delicate a task; and second the fact of my being a foreign student would necessarily put me to much effort to write even a little book in the English language. But the encouragement and prayers of my classmates were such that I could not help but find my needed inspiration and enthusiasm. I ventured upon the task, and this little book is the result.

THE ANGEL IN EBONY

In the preparation of this little volume, I have had to interview several people who personally knew Sammy Morris. I am glad that most of them are still living, and able to help perpetuate, at least, some of the episodes that are so interesting a part of the life of the African youth. But I owe special gratitude for most of my materials to Dr. Harriet Stemen-Macbeth of Ft. Wayne, one of Sammy's teachers, whose parents gave no little help and care when Sammy was at Taylor University; to Mr. Lindley Baldwin of the same city, a choice friend of Doctor Thaddeus C. Reade, and one of those who had developed a fatherly contact with Sammy; to Miss Grace Husted of Greenfield, Indiana, who knew Sammy well, as she had been especially employed by the college authorities to serve as a teacher to Sammy and an Armenian boy. I also wish to extend my thanks to Doctor Burt W. Ayres for helping me solve some of the intricate problems that presented themselves in my investigation of Sammy's religious experiences; and also to Dr. Herbert T. Blodgett and Professor Grace Leal Crozier for their literary criticisms and suggestions. I am indebted to the authorities of Saint Joseph's Hospital for the record of Sammy's illness in the hospital; to the Board of Foreign Missions of the Protestant Episcopal Church for the cut of the West African scene; and to Mr. and Mrs. Robertson of Fort Wayne for the picture of the Berry Street Methodist Church. Most of all I wish to express my sincere appreciation for the way my classmates have supported me in prayer and encouragement.

Jorge O. Masa,
Taylor University
Upland, Indiana
May, 1928.

THE ANGEL IN EBONY

JORGE MASA
Author, Angel in Ebony

INTRODUCTION

The author of this volume will be remembered by his colleagues as a very interesting man. His friends in Taylor University will appreciate some record of his life to be preserved in connection with that of Sammy Morris.

Jorge Masa came with his little wife to the campus of Taylor University four years ago. During this period there was born to them a daughter, Eugenia. They have proved to be a very interesting family, much appreciated by their neighbors. Mr. Masa has had calls in many directions to render service for inspirational missionary meetings among the churches.

Born in a town some 300 miles south of Manila about twenty-six years ago, he is a product of the public school system which was established in his native land by the American government. Finishing secondary school, he did some work in the University of the Philippines before coming to the United States. Though reared in a Catholic land, his parents maintained only a nominal allegiance to the Roman Catholic Church, becoming members of the Philippine Independent Catholic Church after the Spanish American war.

His desire to come to America was fostered by a graduate of Taylor University who was operating in the Philippine field, and he was encouraged to come to Taylor for his higher education "for one great reason, that it is a clean school, from the moral standpoint, and is free from race prejudice of any kind."

With his aims directed toward the medical profession, Mr. Masa came to America and to his alma mater with "a bitter antagonism," using his own expression, "to anything that had a religious element in it." Naturally he was shy of the spiritual influences at Taylor and not entirely satisfied with the first impressions. But to his mind there was power in friendship. The friendly atmosphere that dominates the student life at Taylor led him to investigate the spiritual force which lay back of it. His mind was philosophical enough to see that there was a reason. He found what he conceived to be the reasons, in the prominence that was given to Jesus Christ, and the simple faith that was reflected in the testimony of his associates.

It was not long until Mr. Masa acquired a new and better view of religion. He says: "The discovery of the vast difference between the Jesus Christ whom I had learned from my parents and the Jesus Christ that Taylor University honors and worships marked the turning point of my life. I yielded my soul to him, and then decided to prepare for a life work that would help my own people in a satisfying discovery of the Savior of men."

THE ANGEL IN EBONY

This volume grew out of an inspirational movement of the 1928 Senior Class of Taylor University. In addition to their other benefactions in behalf of their alma mater this class erected a new tomb at Fort Wayne, Indiana, in memory of the interesting colored "Prince Kaboo," whose American name was Samuel Morris. During this enterprise they generated a large interest in the biography of this remarkable boy, having come in contact with an amount of data upon his life not included in the interesting Sammy Morris pamphlet from the pen of Dr. Thaddeus C. Reade a third of a century ago. The lot fell upon Jorge O. Masa to do, in the name of the class, the excellent piece of biographical work here presented. Although English is not Mr. Masa's mother tongue, the reader of these pages will be impressed with his entertaining and eloquent use of the language. By many measurements it is a successful biography. It may appropriately represent the beginning of Mr.

THE ANGEL IN EBONY

Masa's wider ministry as he bids farewell to his college days and turns his face toward the world service which is symbolized by the diploma he has taken.

After the completion of this volume it was our privilege to assist the class at the unveiling of the new monument to Samuel Morris on the afternoon of May 20, 1928. Though some thirty-five years had elapsed since the death of this humble Spirit filled negro, nearly five hundred people assembled to witness the unveiling of the monument. Though many colored people were present, the white citizens were in the majority. It indicates the lasting charm of a consecrated life that exalts the simplicity of the gospel. It warrants us in expecting that the smaller volume which had a sale of more than two hundred thousand and continues in demand will probably be equaled in popularity by "The Angel in Ebony."

John Paul

TAYLOR UNIVERSITY
AT FORT WAYNE

ST. JOSEPH HOSPITAL

THE ANGEL IN EBONY

CHAPTER 1
The Bitter Cup of Childhood

In the western section of Fort Wayne's beautiful Lindenwood cemetery, upon a spot where in summer the spreading branches of luxuriant trees cast their restful shade, once stood a little tombstone, sixteen inches long, twelve inches wide, and two inches thick, with this inscription upon its mossy face:

Samuel Morris
Native of Africa
Born 1873
Died
May 12, 1893
while attending Taylor University
at Fort Wayne, Ind.
preparing himself
for missionary
work among his
own people

THE ANGEL IN EBONY

With costly mausoleums, and stately monuments in their granite eminence proudly rising in the background one would suppose that this little grave with its humble mark had no friends, no admirers to place wreaths as tokens of respect and loving regard for him whose remains lie below. But an inquiry of the cemetery superintendent would reveal the fact that every year approximately five hundred visitors come to see this insignificant resting place and voice their love for Samuel Morris in terms of tears and prayers.

Paradoxical, indeed, that such an insignificant spot, among vaunting marbles, should hold a hallowed place in the hearts of so many people! The fact that the remains are those of a colored boy, who, if living today, would be despised by many a proud and haughty Nordic soul, presents a seeming contradiction in life. But how came it, one would ask, that the memory of his life is being carried in the hearts of so many people?

Samuel Morris was an African of the Africans. He had a skin that was as dusky as the midnight gloom. His lips were thick and protruding, his nose flat and snubby, and his eyes full dark black. Comeliness had no place in his physical bearing. Born in the jungles of Africa, brought up in a heathen environment, foreign to the ways of civilization, he lived and had his being in a strange land of loneliness.

The little stretch of land in the interior of Liberia somewhere between the river Sestas and Grand Sisters was the original home of Samuel Morris.* There in 1873 in the wilds of African forests, upon a bed of grasses and sticks he was born amidst the happy rejoicing of his people who took special delight in the birth of a male. His father was the chief, or King, of the Kroo tribe -- the seamen of Africa. That his people were honest, loyal, courageous, friendly and brave, is not to be questioned, for travelers and missionaries who have gone through that section of the continent testify to the fact.

Originally, Samuel Morris' name was "Kaboo", the meaning of which is hard to determine. But it is the common practice among the tribes in that section of the continent to name a child after some object or circumstance peculiar at the time of his birth, and the recognition of man's superiority and authority in domestic and tribal affairs suggests that in some way he may have been named after some fetish, or after his father, or one of his ancestors.**

To recount his early life is to discuss a pathetic and compassionate theme; for Sammy Morris, unlike most American children, had never tasted the sweet cup of babyhood and childhood. Naked he was born, and naked he grew up.

THE ANGEL IN EBONY

As to his mother, her perverted heart failed
to give him the loving tenderness, and
the blessings which should have been his.
His boyhood days never experienced hallowed moments with a mother who could
teach him to pray in childhood faith; point
him to the eternal stars as the handwrit-
ing of an Infinite God; place a goodnight
kiss upon his dark cheeks at bedtime; or
breathe, "God be with you" when he went
fishing, hunting, or digging roots. He never
knew what it meant to sit beside his father
at eventime and hear him relate such
stories of heroism as would have awakened the slumbering energies of his youth.
Virtue then he hardly knew, for savage
as his people were, they knew nothing of
life save the faint whisper of their brutish
instincts.

Sammy had no shoes to protect his feet
from the deadly thorns of the jungles and
the burning sands of the tropics. He wore

no clothing to keep his black skin from the cruel heat of the torrid sun. He lived and grew a total stranger to the delicacies which are conducive to the normal growth of physical being.

His father was a warlike chief, who had seen many a victory in various engagements with the neighboring tribes, and these victories gave him a name at once formidable and inspiring. But this did not mean that he was no longer threatened. The combined power of several neighboring chiefs attacked him one day and waged a battle which culminated in his utter defeat. His entire kingdom was devastated by his enemies who plundered the whole tribe, killed numbers of women and children, and carried away a host of captives among whom was Samuel Morris.

The lad was barely old enough to remember all that transpired at the time the great misfortune overtook his father's tribe.

THE ANGEL IN EBONY

Being the son of a tribal chief he was not driven to slavery like the rest of the captives, but he was dragged into bondage, treated as a cheap commodity, and looked upon as a pawn, a form of security. That he suffered greatly, is not to be doubted.

Finally, with a heart for the child that was his, the father came to redeem him. The offer was accepted and he took Sammy back to the scene of his childhood, where his mother sat in tears waiting for his return. The village and hut which he had known were gone. No more was heard jubilant laughter in his father's little kingdom. The herds were gone; the patch of field where the men and women had labored to keep the wolf from the village door was razed, devastated, and plundered. Defeat and humiliation enveloped the entire scene.

With his people in such a situation, one would suppose that there were no more grounds for his father's enemies to again torment him. But such was not the case. The victors, in their desire to maintain their position, formulated new plans. What Bismark did for France after the Franco-Prussian War of 1870, the enemies of Sammy's father did for the Kroo tribe. Foreign to the language of mercy and deaf to the voice of compassion, they constantly threatened and annoyed the tribe by imposing upon them heavy tribute, or by burning their fields and produce, thus keeping them in a state of helpless subjection.

The final blow came to the Kroo tribe when Sammy was about eleven years of age. In order to prevent the tribe from ever rising again to power, the whole group was scattered, men were killed, women and children were driven into slavery, and Sammy again found himself in pawn. He had a vivid recollection of that terrible bondage. His captors brutally inflicted upon him cruelties that were even worse than death itself. Every day he was led into the execution field, for savages are not without them, and there before the eyes of his own captive people, he was beaten, not with a stick, but with a long thorny vine, while the tormentors fiendishly shrieked and yelled. After each day's program was completed one captive would be released, who of course would return to Sammy's father with the news of the treatment which Sammy was receiving.

One day his father arrived to redeem him, but the price he offered: ivory, the kernels of palm nuts, and India rubber, along with his younger sister who was of insignificant value to her people on account of her sex, was not sufficient ransom. Sammy, whose heart was instinctively tender, begged to endure the hardships himself rather than see his sister subjected to them. Hence no agreement was reached, and Sammy remained in pawn.

The events that followed are too horrible to describe. Only those who understand the heart of a savage heathen can imagine them. Quoting Sammy's own words: "The cruel man whipped me every day. He whipped me without cause and every day the whipping got harder." Naked and young as he was it is strange that he did not succumb, for greenish-black bleeding stripes made by poisonous thorny vines were daily laid upon his quivering back. He did become so weak that he was unable to walk. Then his persecutors placed him in stocks which they erected. A few yards directly in front of him they dug a hole as a challenge to indicate that if his father failed to bring the required articles for redemption, Sammy would be buried there.

Then the supernatural intervened. By

some strange power, which his heathen mind could not comprehend, suddenly there flashed through his poor, weak, and tortured body an inflow of strength that gave him the boldness to attempt escape. Extricating himself, he fled from the ex-ecution ground into the forest, unmindful of any destination. When his escape was discovered, the whole village ran in search of him, but Sammy was not to be found.

In the wilderness where tigers, lions, snakes, and gorillas were plentiful, he wan-dered, -- alone, hungry, and perplexed. Fearing that his captors were pursuing him, he slept during the daytime in the hollows of giant trees, and recommenced his wanderings when total darkness had gathered around the thick African forest.

Just how many days it took him to com-plete his perilous escape, he could not re-member, although it seemed to him a long, long journey. When he reached the coast

of Liberia, no mother's arms were opened
to welcome him, no tears of joy flowed
from friendly eyes because he had escaped.
His father was not there to rejoice over his
deliverance. There was no friendly face to
encourage him; no one to whom he could
pour out the bursting agonies of his soul
and thus relieve the pangs of his terrible
suffering.

However, in the face of that heart-rending
solitude, he felt that the odds were not
against him. The influence of that
moment, when strength took possession of
his famished soul, and gave him boldness
to escape from his oppressors, remained as
a source of comfort to him, although his
mind, saturated with the perversions of
fetish beliefs could not comprehend it. It
was mysterious but it was real. He held to
it; rejoiced in it; found solace in it.

Going to a coffee plantation he secured
work and board, and received several

articles of clothing, which it was customary for white men to give to their laborers. A new day was beginning for Sammy Morris.

*Encyclopaedia Britannica, Vol. 16, 1911, P. 542.

**W. H. Kelsey -- West African Studies, MacMillan, 1899--603-604.

Dr. Idora Rose
Dr. Harriet Macbeth   Miss Grace Husted

CHAPTER II
The Turning Point

The plantation where Sammy worked was situated not far from the town of Monrovia, the present capital city of the Liberian republic. The plantation may have been owned either by an Englishman, or by a Portuguese who at that time was enjoying himself in profits at the expense of negro labor. But to one like Samuel Morris who had just undergone terrible persecution, it was most satisfactory. He was happy to have a job, and realized nothing of the harmful exploitation of his rights. The stripes of the cruel man's whip were still on his back, and the memory of painful hours was still fresh in his mind, causing him to joyfully appreciate his new plantation employment. Here he found good clothing, and other necessities of physical life. All that he needed to do to please his masters was to work hard, and that was not difficult for him. Born and reared in the sweltering heat of the torrid African climate, he could stand the hottest days and the hardest kind of work.

It was here on the plantation that light began to gleam across his pathway. He became friendly with a boy, perhaps of the Kroo tribe, who unfolded to him one day the happy secret of his soul, a secret which started Sammy in quest of a similar experience in his own life. The hallowed moment of his escape began to take new meaning.

This Christian friend invited Sammy to accompany him the next Sunday to church. He went, and what a strange coincidence of events. On that very day, Miss Knolls, a native of Fort Wayne, Indiana, educated at Fort Wayne Methodist Episcopal College, was present as a missionary. She was scheduled to speak, through an interpreter, on the conversion of St. Paul.

THE ANGEL IN EBONY

The story of the man of Tarsus gripped the heart of the poor colored boy, who knowing nothing of the meaning of God's love, of Jesus Christ, or of the Holy Spirit, shouted "That's just what I saw; that was what brought me here and saved me from my oppressors."

Whether Miss Knolls was disturbed or not in her talk, it cannot be said but the whole congregation was startled. Sammy was wild with joy. He returned home that evening possessed of a deep conviction that the light which had prostrated Paul and his companions on the Syrian road emanated from the same Source which had given him strength to escape his terrible persecution. It is evident that these experiences are not on the same plane. His was more of a release, a deliverance from a bondage, while that of Paul's was a discipline, a subjection, with the end in view of revealing him as one fighting against God and His divine purposes. Nevertheless, to a simple mind like Sammy's a mind devoid of any critical attitude, experiences similar to those of the man of Tarsus only enriched his life and increased his knowledge of God.

In Paul's conversion Sammy saw the Holy Grail of his soul. God, a real God, the God for whom he was feebly groping the God whom his people have been struggling to worship in terms of magic and taboo -- that God became a reality to him. He found that He was not distant, nor inaccessible; not an impersonal spirit dwelling in the hollows of trees, in a stick, in a parrot's feather, a root, a claw, a seed or any other curious or conspicuous object. On the other hand, he learned that He is a Person, great enough and good enough to deliver him from his miseries and sufferings, and to diffuse through his soul the fragrance of a new assurance, an assurance that builds hope and ushers in peace.

The days that followed were days of spiritual and moral victories. Constantly, whether at work or at rest, his eyes were fixed on Jesus. He could not escape Him. That he might know more of Him, Sammy attended church services every Sunday, and frequently visited Miss Knolls, who gladly helped him in his time of need. She taught him to read and write the English language, and gave him brief and fragmentary lessons in the Bible. Thus he gradually became acquainted with his Savior and Master. He grew in strength and grace day by day, and felt the world around him taking a different aspect and newer meaning. Everything seemed to grow bright and glorious. Hum-drum, drudgery, and hardship disappeared from his life. The commonplace was removed. "Everything swung around into a new setting." All things seemed to adjust themselves for his benefit.

In addition to the Bible instruction, Miss Knolls taught him to pray. This he called "talking to his Father." With that interpretation as a starting point, he developed a wonderful prayer life, which in the days that followed, became the power and glory of his personality. He would at all times, when there was a sense of need in his heart, pray to Him whom he loved. Often he would break the hush of midnight with his prayers, and often provoked the indignation of his soundly sleeping fellow workmen. Rebuked for his unseasonable times of prayer, and admonished that if he persisted he would be driven away like a dog, Sammy transferred his altar of prayer to the woods. There night after night he wrestled with angels. There with a simple yet firm trust in the farseeing Providence whose Fatherly care he believed was ever around him, whose responsiveness was the responsiveness of one who is sensitive to the slightest appeal, and whose kindness would keep back no good thing that He could bestow, -- there night after night he burst into agonies that bespoke the depth of his thanksgiving and the great earnestness of his supplications.

Why he was called Samuel Morris is a question that has hitherto been unanswered. Although Doctor Reade and the Reverend Stephen Merritt are silent on this matter in the biographies which they wrote, the question need not remain unanswered. The lady, who gave him instruction in reading and writing, taught him the simple lessons of the gospel and revealed to him Jesus Christ, was the one who changed his name from "Kaboo" to Samuel Morris. A study of her life at Fort Wayne College will explain why she did this. Miss Knolls did not come from wealthy parents. Reared in the city of

Fort Wayne, she was educated in its public schools and at the Methodist Episcopal College. That she was a promising student, possessed of high and lofty ideals, is not to be questioned; otherwise she could not have gained the interest of a well-to-do banker and philanthropist who paid most of her college expenses and inspired her to dedicate her life to Christian service abroad.

When she was graduated from college, she asked to be sent to Africa as a missionary; and being an alumnus of the school that had felt the saintly touch of Bishop William Taylor, she was accepted and sent out at once. She landed in Liberia and there brought to herself a name and glory by making Prince Kaboo the first fruit. To indicate her deep loyalty and gratitude to the Fort Wayne banker who made possible her education, she named her convert Samuel Morris after him.

Sammy did not stay long at the plantation. He went to Monrovia and began a job of painting. Reverend Arthur Jordan, who has been a missionary in Liberia since 1912, had the privilege of knowing a member of the crew in the gunboat of the Liberian navy who told him that he had worked with Sammy for a month, painting the Liberian College of Monrovia. He took a vital interest in missionary services among the citizens of Monrovia, a work which is beautifully reflected in the following episode.

Nancy Minor, a worker among the Kroo tribe, and two native women, were anxious to see the whole community accept Jesus Christ as its Savior. To carry out their plans, they agreed to conduct prayer meetings starting at midnight and lasting until daylight which continued for months. One dark still night the three devout workers were joined by a native boy who silently entered and prostrated himself near the pulpit, where he prayed for hours. Leaving him undisturbed, the women went from door to door, breaking the good news to other church members. When they returned, they discovered that the boy was none other than Sammy Morris who had come, not to find Jesus Christ for himself, but to pray that others might know his "Father." Their united prayers were not without fruit. The spirit of the lowly Nazarene moved upon the whole community, and fifty young people were brought to know that abundant life through Christ Jesus.

The chief concern in Sammy's heart was to have others know his Father. He had felt in his soul man's utter need of a Savior and Redeemer. To Sammy, the life which he lived in Christ seemed different from that lived by thousands around him. Sammy had a calm and settled peace in

his soul. The dawning of each day brought
a new supply of joy and gladness to him.
Life was all meaningful; it was abundant.
Love had laid hold upon him.

But around him was a desolate picture
of sin and bondage. It was a fact which
he could not escape. He had to face it.
Little children in their mournful sobs,
desperately crying for love; manhood and
womanhood crucified on the iron cross
of meaningless life, -- these things profoundly stirred his inmost soul, and his
throat became dry, his eyes grew moist.
The burden assumed an intense weight
which he was unable to endure. He trav-
eled many miles to take part in the labors
of the Revered C.E. Smirl, hoping to gain
relief. "You must be educated in order to
serve your people," advised Mr. Smirl.

"How can I be educated?" he asked.

"You must go to America," was the reply.

THE ANGEL IN EBONY

Little did Sammy realize the full import of that declaration. Going to America meant an expense of a hundred dollars, and Sammy, poor as he was, was perplexed. That night he tarried for many hours in the woods, and prayed his Father to make a way for him. "Father," he cried, "the missionary told me that I must be educated; and to be educated I must go to America. How can I, for I do not have the hundred dollars to pay?"

Leaving the woods just before daybreak he had an assurance that his Father would prepare a way. Day after day he lay in wait for a ship that would take him to America. Meanwhile he felt a great desire to know more about the land to which he was going. He became acquainted with a missionary by the name of Lizzie MacNeil who had come to Africa largely through the influence and help of Stephen Merritt, former secretary [sic] to Bishop William

Taylor. Miss MacNeil took a deep interest in Sammy.

One day this new friend told him about the Comforter, who, as she said, is the Holy Spirit of God, manifesting Himself in the hearts of those who believe in Jesus Christ. Sammy was puzzled the first time he heard her message, but it interested him. Her explanation did not satisfy the lad who was "hungering after righteousness", and in her utter helplessness she advised him to go to Stephen Merritt for further information.

"Where is Stephen Merritt?" he asked.

"In New York City."

With the words, "I will see him," Sammy slipped away and ran toward the shore, where he saw a vessel bound for America. His joy knew no limits. He was going to America to see Stephen Merritt and to be educated.

BERRY STREET M. E. CHURCH,
FORT WAYNE

CHAPTER III
The Angel in Ebony

The departure of Sammy Morris from his native land was colored with a strange blending of faith, pathos, and humor. When he left Lizzie MacNeil, telling her that he was going to New York, he did not realize the vast difficulties before him. He took it for granted that going to New York City was just like going to an African village, and seeing Stephen Merritt like seeing one of the missionaries in Monrovia. He had no learning, save to read and write a few English words. He had no idea of the miseries of an ocean voyage; of the risk involved in crossing the vast Atlantic in a small sailing vessel; he did not conceive of sea-sickness which is commonly the lot of ocean travelers.

The boat which dropped anchor nearby when Sammy reached the shore was one of those tramp vessels which were

49

a common sight along the African coast in those days. It did not run under any regular line, but took cargo wherever the captain, who owned and dominated its affairs, desired. The life on board was marked by utter hardness and cruelty. Every word spoken was emphasized with cuffs and curses. From captain down to the lowest servant, they were slaves to violence.

When the captain landed, Sammy, with a great deal of confidence stepped up to him and asked if he would take him to New York. He was denied with kicks and cuffs and curses. He could not endure it. He cried and wondered why such was his treatment. With these thoughts in his mind, he lay down on the sand and slept. In the meantime the captain had returned to the ship; but in the morning he put to shore again, and Sammy, anxious and determined to go to New York, approached with his former request. The captain, who was too busy to pay attention to the pleading of the poor colored boy, turned and threatened to kick him.

Throughout that day Sammy wandered along the shore heartbroken and sad. The ship was still there and the men were still loading cargoes. He slept again that night on the sand; when morning came he approached the captain a third time and presented his request. As two men had deserted and as Sammy was understood to be a Kroo boy, the captain, instead of cursing him and kicking him, asked "What do you want?" meaning pay.

Sammy whose knowledge of the English language was limited, answered, "I want to see Stephen Merritt."

The captain who hardly had time to ask further questions ordered the men on the boat to take the boy aboard. Imagine his joy! At last he was going to see Stephen

Merritt. There was a song and a shout; praise filled his soul. His "Father" had answered his prayer.

In the afternoon the boat set sail. Sammy was to leave Africa, his native land! But little did he realize the significance of his departure. There was pathos in the scene. Not a soul on the shore uttered a word of good-bye and Godspeed to him. His mother was not there to give him her last tearful kiss of farewell; there was absent the figure of a father to speak words of counsel. Gradually as the boat ploughed through the water, he saw his native land slowly fade in the distance. In his soul the love of country was undeveloped.

The first days on the ocean were hard days for Sammy. He was sea-sick. One day, as he was lying in the gunwale terribly sick and almost lifeless, the captain discovered him and was so very angry that he almost threw him overboard. In the midst of his utter distress, when no food or care was given him, he calmly looked up to his 'Father" [sic] and silently uttered pleadings for help. The next day one of the crew came to him and said, "Cuff," (a cognomen applied to him in view of his severe treatment from the captain) "if you will do my work, I will do yours." His work was to make up the Captain's bunk and clean up the cabin. Sammy went down to that work, and the man stayed on the deck. When the captain saw Sammy, he was so indignant that he struck him with his fist. Sammy, who was weak and utterly bewildered, fell on the floor almost unconscious. When he came to himself, he rose and with eyes that beamed with tenderness and love, asked the captain if he knew Jesus. His master had heard of Christ in his boyhood days, for his mother was a Christian woman; but he ran away from home early in his life and since then had been under such a spell of brutal ocean life that he scarcely knew the name that Sammy had uttered. The captain, moved by some mysterious power, fell beside his bunk while Sammy pointed him to "the Lamb of God which taketh away the sins of the world." The cruel man, harsh and rough, saw a vision of his lost condition. The "deep had spoken unto the deep," and life became meaningful again. Before the vessel was halfway across the Atlantic, nearly all the crew underwent the captain's glorious experience. "One loving soul had set others on fire."

One night a storm swept the ocean, and the small vessel was tossed up and down. Sammy was busy with his job, and as the winds roared through the rigging and the water dashed fiercely against the side of the vessel, the crew from the deck could hear the earnest prayers of the African boy, breaking through the noise of the waves. That was enough for them. Sammy knew his "Father" would heed his cry. The next morning, all was calm and still, and the little vessel was moving through the deep, sailing steadily on a smooth ocean.

Sammy had all his belongings in a little piece of handkerchief when he went on board. When the vessel arrived at the foot of Day Street, New York, he had a sailor's bag full of clothing and presents from the crew. He landed without a cent in his pocket, without a friend to greet him, and without a home to which to go. He stepped up to the first man on the dock and asked, "Where is Stephen Merritt?" Fortunately, however, the man was a member of the Traveler's Aid Club, and Stephen Merritt being connected with that organization was known to him.

"He is three miles away," was the reply. "I will take you to him for a dollar." So Sammy picked up his sailor's bag and followed the man. It was almost evening time when they reached their destination. Stephen Merritt was then pastor of the St. James Street Methodist Episcopal Church, and when Sammy came, he was starting for prayer meeting.

"There is Stephen Merritt," pointed the man.

"Stephen Merritt," called Sammy, "I have come from Africa to talk to you about the Holy Spirit."

"Have you any letter of recommendation?" he was asked. But Sammy with a glad look replied, "No. I have Him, and He will introduce me to you." Just as Merritt was about to send him to the mission which was next door to his office, the member of the Traveler's Aid interrupted, "Where is my one dollar?"

"Oh, Stephen Merritt pays all my expenses now," Sammy answered. And Mr. Merritt gave the man one dollar saying,

"Surely, I pay all his expenses now."

He was sent to the mission where a friend in charge was instructed to keep him until Stephen Merritt returned. But it was not until after eleven o'clock at night when Mr. Merritt got back. He had been delayed partly because his prayer meeting had such extraordinary spiritual intensity that nearly all were oblivious of the time, and partly because he almost forgot Sammy himself. He had been arrested several times for keeping the meeting open and the judge had let him go with the understanding that he was to close his meeting in the mission at eleven o'clock sharp.

Just as he was on his way home, the thought of Sammy Morris struck him, and at once, he ran to the mission. He expected an arrest, for then it was past eleven. When he reached the place, he found seventeen men on their knees, while Sammy knelt in their midst. The great deeps were broken up. Something profound had stirred their inmost being. Their very souls had been touched and they felt the need of a saving God, all because of the poor yet earnest African boy.

Stephen Merritt took the boy to his home; and when he opened the door, his wife, who had been anxious about him, asked, "What have you got there?"

"Oh, Dolly," he replied, "An Angel in Ebony."

She was astonished! "What are you going to do with him?" she asked.

"I am going to put him in the Bishop's bed."*

"No, don't."

"I will."

He took Sammy to the Bishop's room, showed him the bed, and instructed him about lighting and putting out the gas, then he went to the bureau drawer in his room and took out one of the night shirts, a new one, and put it on Sammy. As the sleeves were altogether too long for him, Stephen Merritt burst into laughter. But just as he was about to leave the room, Sammy held him by the hand and asked him to kneel with him. The laughter was transformed to tears. Stephen Merritt, the man who had been preaching the Gospel of Christ for years; the man whom Bishop William Taylor had selected to be his secretary met God as never before in that few minutes' prayer with the poor colored Kroo boy.

The following morning, when Mr. Merritt returned home from his early morning walk to supervise the work of the men in the mission, he found Sammy at the table with Mrs. Merritt, who was in tears, a rather unusual circumstance, for she was

one of those women who are good but
not compassionate. "Brother Morris," she
said, "you ask the blessing." And Sammy
stretched out his arms and uttered a
simple thanksgiving that made his host
and hostess break again into tears. "Anything you want, anything you desire, we
will give you. Make your home here," Mrs.
Merritt said.

One day Sammy was taken in a coach
to Harlem where Mr. Merritt was to of-
ficiate at the funeral of one of his church
memebrs [sic]. On their way, thinking
Sammy would be interested in the unique
sights of the city, Mr. Merritt showed
him the opera house, business buildings,
and parks; but suddenly Sammy took his
hand and begged to kneel with him in
the coach. He knelt and told his "Father"
that probably he was mistaken in going
to Stephen Merritt; for until then his host
had not talked to him about the Holy

Spirit, to learn of whom, Sammy had crossed the Atlantic. Then he begged his "Father" to touch the lips of Stephen Merritt so that he could never preach on any subject but Jesus Christ and the Holy Spirit. It was a simple prayer, but its profound earnestness carried with it conviction that Stephen Merritt could not resist. The "Angel in Ebony" had brought him more deeply and fully into the knowledge and love of God.

His presence in the funeral service was so beautiful that there beside the casket three men fell on their knees and saw for the first time the value of a life that is within the love of Jesus Christ.

He was taken to church on Sunday afternoon. It was announced before hand that he was coming to speak to the Sunday School about the Holy Spirit, so that some six hundred people were present to hear him. "I have one with me," introduced

Stephen Merritt, "Samuel Morris of Africa. He came to talk to you about the Holy Ghost."

When his name was announced, he arose, went forward, and leaned against the altar rail. Just what he said, Stephen Merritt himself could not recall, but the boy in ebony made the entire congregation feel that they were on sacred ground; God was there. There was meekness, there was tenderness, there was persuasiveness, there was that touch of heavenly love in his soul, that in him the people saw the uplifted Christ. The Sunday School was forgotten. Men and women, teachers and pupils, all dropped on their knees.

On one side of the room a group gathered and inaugurated what later proved to be a Sammy Morris Missionary Society. At the suggestion of Stephen Merritt, it was resolved that Sammy be sent to Taylor University, Fort Wayne, Indiana, where he might secure the necessary preparation for his future work among his own people. And Taylor University was just the place for him; for there, even as now, its atmosphere, infused with the world vision and spiritual influence of its namesake, Bishop William Taylor, tended to promote the cultivation of genuine fellowship and the development of that mystical attitude which was already manifest in Sammy's soul.

Three days later Stephen Merritt took Sammy to the depot where he boarded a train for Fort Wayne. With him were three trunks of necessities that the society which bore his name had given him.

*Stephen Merritt was Bishop William Taylor's home secretary, and when he was in New York City he made Stephen Merritt's home his lodging place.

VIEWS OF TAYLOR UNIVERSITY,
UPLAND, INDIANA

CHAPTER IV
The Irresistible Personality

The brief sojourn of Sammy Morris in
New York City proved a blessing to the
members of James Street Church. No
less than ten thousand conversions took
place between that time and the end of
Stephen Merritt's pastorate -- conversions that might not have occurred apart
from the marvelous spiritual impact of the
"Angel in Ebony." The congregation had
known what Christianity is in its relation
to the human soul and the world; and had
understood the mission of Jesus Christ to
the spiritual and moral life of men; but it
was not until they saw the poor but earnest
figure of Sammy Morris and heard his
broken yet irresistible message, that the
reality of the religion they professed was
unfolded to them. The poor African had
pointed them to the Way, the Truth, and
the Life.

Stephen Merritt, testifying to the influence of Sammy's life upon himself wrote: "Bishops have placed their hands on my head once and again, and joined with elders of the church in ordaining services, but no power came in comparison. James Caughey placed his holy hands on my head and on the head of dear Thomas Harrison as he prayed that the mantle of Elijah might fall upon the Elishas -- and the fire fell and the power came; but the abiding Comforter was received in the coach with Samuel Morris -- for since then I have not written a line or spoken a word, or preached a sermon only for or in the Holy Ghost."

At the time Sammy entered Taylor University, the school was facing a financial crisis, a situation which had always been in its lot. However, Doctor Thaddeus C. Reade, then its president, in consultation with Doctor C. B. Stemen, an honored

phyiscian [sic] and distinguished citizen
of Fort Wayne, who had previously been
president of the college, felt that if Sammy
were what Stephen Merritt had told him
his coming would mean a spiritual blessing
to the school and an asset to the life of the
student body as a whole.

Upon his arrival he was met by Doctor
Stemen, who took a very great interest in
him; for in Sammy he saw his opportunity
to realize, at least in part, his early dreams
of investing his life as a medical missionary to Africa. He took Sammy to his home
where he stayed for two weeks until the
school opened.

Curiosity was great on Sammy's own part,
for everything was new to him. He had to
be introduced to his clothes, and become
acquainted with the food, and learn how
to eat it properly. Once when the teacher
in charge of the Art Department request-
ed him to pose in the studio, as her class

wished to draw his picture, he surprised
her with a frank refusal, explaining that
he could not bear to stay in that room
because it contained strange white heads,
white hands and white feet. When told
that they were only plaster casts, he said
that it made no difference, for he dreaded
to look at them. But he consented when
asked if he would be willing to sit for the
class in some other room. So the students
took him into the room across the hall
from the studio. There he posed patiently
until they completed an excellent portrait
of him.

On another occasion, the back of his hand
was hurt, and the outer skin removed;
the color underneath was a shade lighter.
He told his teacher that he put ink on it
because he was afraid it might turn white
and be a disgrace to him forever, should he
go back to Africa with a white spot on his
hand.

THE ANGEL IN EBONY

On a Thanksgiving Day at the home of Doctor Reade, he was asked which country he liked best -- a question frequently asked of foreign students, by Americans. He answered them by asking another question, "What is better, roast turkey or raw monkey?"

"Why Sammy!" remarked Doctor Reade seriously, "You didn't eat monkeys?"

"Oh, yes," he replied, "I ate monkeys and ate them raw."

When the warm spring weather had come his teacher put on a white dress one morning and went to her classroom. Sammy was waiting there. He looked up as she entered and much surprised at her appearance. He began to laugh aloud and asked, "Why, do folks in this country wear clothes all summer?" The question of course contained no suggestion of rudeness. He merely noticed the difference between the customs of America and Africa.

However, in spite of Sammy's odd ways, he was well treated and much respected. "I wish to say here," wrote President Reade, commenting on Sammy Morris as the first colored student in the school, "to the honor of the faculty and students of the University, if he had been the President's son he could not have been treated with greater courtesy. He was loved and respected by all."

When asked one time what room he wanted, he looked up into the President's face and with a smile pervaded with humility and tenderness said, "Oh, Mr. Reade, any room is good enough for me. If there is a room nobody wants, give that to me." This was too much for a Christian of Doctor Reade's makeup. "I turned away," he wrote, "for my eyes were full of tears. I was asking myself whether I was willing to take what nobody else wanted. In my experiences as a teacher, I have had occasion to assign rooms to more than a thousand pupils. Most of them were noble, Christian young ladies and gentlemen, but Sammy Morris was the only one of them who ever said, 'If there is a room that nobody wants, give that to me.'"

Shortly after his arrival, Doctor Reade, anxious to make Sammy and the problem of his maintenance known to a host of interested friends, wrote an Advocate which brought in thirteen dollars which was used in fitting up his room and in buying his books.

His studies at Fort Wayne were entirely primary, for he scarcely knew how to read and write. Dr. Stemen's daughter, now Dr. Harriet Macbeth, with another lady who is at present a physician in a Presbyterian hospital at Chicago under the professional name of Dr. Idora Rose, bent over Sammy to give him his daily lessons. The work was hard for them both, and they were at that time pursuing their medical courses; but the enthusiasm of their pupil was something they could not help but encourage.

It might be mentioned that in these daily lessons Sammy would never enter into his work without spending some time in talking to his "Father." It did not matter to him whether his teachers were already in the room waiting for him to begin his lessons; he had to speak to Him first, a talk which very often consumed half an hour or more. But his strength and enthusiasm, his interest and earnestness, were derived from those quiet moments when he lost himself completely in the love and will of God. His very life was drawn from his contact with his "Father." Apart from that all seemed impossible to him.

Sammy's arrival was followed by a letter from a certain young Dr. Walker of New

York who wrote of a young Armenian, whose mother was a Bible woman in Turkey. He had come to America to be educated that he might help his mother in the work of spreading the Gospel among their people. He landed in Castle Garden without a friend or a dollar, and with very little knowledge of the English language. Doctor Walker thought immediately of sending him to Taylor University. The Faith Fund, which was started at the coming of Sammy Morris to Taylor University, made it possible for the college authorities to take the Armenian boy. When he arrived they secured the services of Miss Grace Husted, whose devotion as a teacher was a living inspiration to the two foreign boys. Speaking of Sammy as her pupil, she has this to say, "He was remarkable for his earnest effort to learn and his undivided attention to every lesson. Having nothing to unlearn, possessing no undue conception of his own importance, he was entirely submissive to the instruction and discipline of the teachers."

"It was a delightful period in the days of class work routine when he entered the class alone, as he was not sufficiently advanced to recite with the other students. For his English lessons the Bible was the text book. Reverently and carefully would he read the chapters assigned. He was so interested in asking questions and in commenting upon the meaning of the text, that the recitation hour was never long enough to satisfy him."

Interesting as these facts of his life at the college are, it was not these things by which Sammy stamped his name on the history of the school. One Sunday morning, not long after he came to Fort Wayne, he went to the African Methodist Episcopal Church of the city. Just as the service was about to commence, Sammy asked the minister to let him speak. The preacher, who was rather a stubborn character and who wanted his own way, was at first reluctant to grant the request of the strange boy. But he confessed later that when he was about to answer in the negative he looked on Sammy's face, and its articulate expression of humility and tenderness was something he could not resist. He gave way and turned over the preaching service to the strange boy. Sammy had hardly said half of what he wanted to tell them, when the eyes of all in the congregation were wet with tears. It was something that had never occurred in the church before.

Sammy's English was broken, and his accents so faulty that it seemed impossible for the congregation to understand him; yet his shining face beaming with the expression of a crucified self, and his solemn figure characterized by total submission to a Higher will, so set fire to their souls that the majestic love of Jesus Christ became real to them.

Sammy was so amiable and friendly to all students in the college that they would often pay him a visit in his room. It was in that fellowship with his visitors that his influence upon the student body as a whole was most deeply felt. For Sammy could find no way to entertain his friends save to ask them to read a passage in the Bible and to spend some few minutes with him in tarrying before his "Father." When one student, who was rather agnostically bent in his religious attitude, came into Sammy's room one day, he told Sammy frankly that he did not believe in the Bible, hence it was impossible for him to spend the hour in Scripture reading and in praying. Sammy was not indignant. He looked into the eyes of his friend, and in a broken exhortation said, "What, you no believe that book! Your Father speak, you no believe him! Your brother speak, you no believe him! The sun shine and you no believe it! God your Father, Christ your brother, the Holy Spirit your Sun. I pray for you." He dropped on his knees and uttered a solemn cry to his Father for his friend, a prayer which lasted for several hours. The visitor left him alone in the room but scarcely had he passed through the door when the sincerity and faith of his black friend found an echo in his soul. Could he remain blind to what he saw? He was not at once converted, but as he pondered on the experiences of his African friend, the deeper the challenge of Christ became to him, until one day he discovered it all vain to deny Him.

One Sunday Doctor Stemen took Sammy to Columbia City that he might bring Sammy's need to the people who were interested in the work of Taylor University. A free-will offering of $11 was made, but Sammy knowing not what it was, turned to Doctor Stemen and with a subdued voice of pain said, "Take me where they speak about Jesus." Doctor Stemen brushed away a tear from his eye. He could not stand so touching an appeal. Sammy struck the keynote of Christ's teaching; "Seek ye first the kingdom of God and all these things shall be added unto you."

Early one morning he surprised Doctor Reade when he asked to quit school that he might go to work. Thinking that Sammy was dissatisfied with his life in the school, Doctor Reade begged him to explain his reason for making a request. "No," Sammy answered, "I love the school very much, but I want to work and get money to bring Henry O'Neil to this country."

"Who is Henry O'Neil?" he was asked.

"Oh, he is my brother in Christ. I led him to Jesus in Africa. He is a good boy; he better than Sammy; he walk close to God. I want him to come here and get an education."

Doctor Reade, in his characteristic fatherly manner said, "Well, Sammy, if he ought to come to America, the Lord will open the way. Talk to your Father about it."

Sammy left the room and spent nearly the whole day in asking his Father to send Henry O'Neil to America. The next day he dropped into the office of the president, and with his face beaming with joy said, "Mr. Reade, I very happy this morning. Father tell me Henry shall come."

Through Mrs. Drake of Illinois, who with her husband, had been a missionary in Africa, Doctor Reade was able to inquire about Henry O'Neil. It was discovered that Henry O'Neil had been in the employ of a certain family, and that measures were already on foot to bring Sammy's friend to America. It is to be regretted however, that Henry O'Neil missed joining Sammy at Fort Wayne. He was sent to St. Louis where he was under the tutorage of a certain Miss Adams, who later sent him to another school. Here he studied for one year, after which he returned to Africa to help his people. He was one of Sammy's first fruits.

Sammy's life at Fort Wayne not only brought a spiritual blessing to the many he met there, but it also proved a living inspiration to all those who were interested in the case of foreign missions. His presence in the student body gave expression to one of the unique ideals of Taylor University -- world evangelism. In him the students found an answer to the question which has been hurled at those who have left home and country that they might witness to the deathless love and life that is in Christ Jesus. In him they profoundly realized the vast significance of the cause for which Bishop William Taylor untiringly dedicated his entire manhood.

Many a time Sammy would go with some of the students for a walk outside of the city. It was these hours, when they would exchange their spiritual experiences and relate their life plans one to the other. That proved especially enriching to all of them. To one of his friends he said, "When I get back to Africa, I will gather the children about me and they will sit on the sand. They will call me father, but I wouldn't care for that, I will tell them of Jesus and some of them will go away in the bushes and I will know what that means -- when they come back they will be very happy."

There was nothing more in the homeland dearer to the heart of Sammy than the children. It is doubtful if he realized the vast possibilities that lie in the lives of young children when it comes to the problem of Christianizing or evangelizing any people or any nation, but instinctively his great soul cried out for them; their helplessness and their innocence was something to which he could not be indifferent. To be a father to them, a real father, by loving and helping them, that was what he longed for. Week in and week out he wove this beautiful dream into his glorious plan of helping his people.

The Berry Street Methodist Church, which once stood on the present site of Anthony Wayne Hotel, was the church to which he belonged. During the long cold winter of 1893 Sammy was a regular attendant at its revival meetings. It did not matter whether the night was dark or stormy or twenty degrees below zero, he felt it his duty to be present. "His honest black face was a benediction; his simple heart yearning for the truth was an inspiration to the minister to do his best to tell the gospel story."

Coming from a continent where snow is unknown and where the climate is a perennial spring and summer; his body, though strong, could not withstand a temperature of twenty or twenty-five degrees below zero. He caught a severe cold in January, 1893, and from that time on, he was unable to get rid of it. Moreover, the American food seemed quite unfitted to his digestion. One day, when he caught hold of a Bible verse on fasting, he began to abstain from food most of the days of the week, until finally his weakened system invited a dropsical condition. Fearing that his sufferings would involve much trouble on the part of the school authorities, he kept silent and bore his sickness as calmly as if nothing was wrong with him. But indications of his difficulty could be readily discerned. His health gradually waned; he could not hide it. His student friends aware of his situation, disclosed the facts to Doctor Reade and Doctor Stemen.

Thereupon he was taken to St. Joseph's Hospital where he received the best of care and treatment. Every day the colored people, who had learned to love him and whose souls had been enriched by his ministry, bought him flowers as a token of their affection. At first Sammy seemed unable to comprehend why he was in this condition of ill health. "I don't understand it," he told his visiting friends. "When I froze my ears last winter they hurt me very much; I asked my Father about it and they quit hurting right away, and now I can't get well. I can't understand it.

But one day when some of the students came in to pay him their daily visit, Sammy revealed to them joyfully, yet with sadness, that he knew it all.

"Oh," he cried, "I am so happy. I understand now. I have seen the angels and they will come for me soon." There was deep pain in the hearts of his visitors. Sammy, their beloved Sammy! Was he going to leave them behind? They left the room with tears in their eyes as he smiled goodbye to them for the last time.

Doctor C. B. Stemen's home was so located, directly across the street from the hospital, that the family was able to extend to Sammy the needed care and attention. Indeed in their devotion Sammy saw the purest embodiment of Christian love and solicitude. On a beautiful afternoon, May 12, as Doctor Stemen was mowing his lawn, he heard a voice exhorting, "Don't work too hard Doctor Stemen." He turned around and saw Sammy looking out of the window with a smile upon his face.

Sammy left the window and reclined once more in his chair; Doctor Stemen returned to his work. A few minutes later however, Sister Helen of the hospital came down to notify the family that Sammy seemed to be entirely helpless. When Doctor Stemen arrived at the hospital the brave young African boy sat lifeless in his chair. He had just passed away. Sammy Morris was dead! A solemn expression of wonderful victory and blessed joy seemed to rest upon his dark cheeks.

Tears, yes tears of sincerest grief were shed by all who were in the death room that glorious May afternoon. Every heart was oppressed with the pain of a great bereavement. Sammy Morris had gone home to meet his "Father."

At the time of his death, Doctor Reade was at Upland, Indiana, where it was planned to move Taylor University in the fall of that year. When he left Fort Wayne, he did not realize that Sammy's illness had reached a critical point. So when the news

was flashed to him that the African boy,
whom he had learned to love as his own
son, had gone, he felt as if a crushing blow
had fallen upon him. He wept and sobbed
like a little child. Samuel Morris was dead;
the wonderful and loving soul, whose
future was all bright with the promise of
hope, whose life had been a benediction
to Taylor University. The grief, the pain,
that throbbed in his heart, he could not
express. When he returned to the campus,
he felt that Sammy's death had left a
vacant place in the school.

The entire student body keenly felt their
loss. There was gloom and depression
in the atmosphere of the school rooms
at the report that Sammy was dead. His
voice, which echoed in prayers in the
silent hours of the night, was to be heard
no more; his solemn and inspiring figure,
which had awakened slumbering souls to
the love and goodness of God, was to be

seen no longer in their midst. Gone: the apostle of simple faith, the angel in ebony, the embodiment of child-like humility.

That they might offer him their last tribute of love, they took turns at night watching around the casket. And here again the wonderful happened. Face to face with the lifeless remains of one whom they had learned to love and to call their own, they began to ponder on the meaning of his short but glorious life. "Why," asked one, "was this life cut so short?"

"Oh," replied another, "there are flowers that are too beautiful to bloom on earth."

Then question after question followed, till Sammy himself was forgotten. Life, death, God, immortality of the soul, these problems took hold of their minds, until finally they returned to the memories of their honored dead whose simple but sublime soul was an answer to all the baffling questions before them. There was sorrow, but there was joy; there was deep grief, but no note of despair. Faith became all triumphant.

Sympathy and love reached their highest point at the funeral where the students tenderly carried his casket from the college to Berry Street Methodist Episcopal Church. Hundreds of mourners stood with bare heads as his casket passed by, and the many that gathered to attend the funeral service were more than the church could hold. In the words of Dr. Reade himself, "It was one of the largest and the most sympathetic funerals I ever witnessed in the city of Fort Wayne."

It is strange that a poor African boy, with thick lips and black face, one whose childhood was spent in the wilds and jungles of the Dark Continent should be so honored and respected by all. Strange that so many eyes were moist when his body was laid to rest beneath the sod. But in Sammy Morris, his beautiful and devoted life, his unquestioning and never dying faith, men saw the vision of the forgiving and transforming Christ. His life was the articulate cry of the human soul for God.

"And when he fell in whirlwind, he went down

As when a lordly cedar, green with boughs,

Goes down with a great shout upon the hills,

And leaves a lonesome place against the sky."

CHAPTER V
Divinely Sent Messenger

On Thursday evening, a week following Sammy's death, the students of the college held their usual prayer meeting. The testimonies that were heard from nearly all the students bore witness to how much the coming of Sammy Morris to Taylor University had meant. It may be said that those testimonies were not simple conventional words; sobs and tears accompanied them, and bespoke the sincerity of hearts that struggled to release their imprisoned affection and gratitude. It cannot be doubted that Sammy's coming to Taylor was providential. Doctor Reade, who keenly sensed this, wrote "Samuel Morris was a divinely-sent messenger of God to touch Taylor University. He thought he was coming over to prepare himself for his mission -- he was coming over to this country to prepare Taylor University for her mission in this world … She got a vision of the world's needs. It was no longer local, but world-wide. Samuel himself was the Macedonian cry, 'Come over and help us,' and a missionary spirit fell upon the school. Since then students have been going to the ends of the world."

The memory of his brief life -- for he was barely twenty at the time of his death -- is something too beautiful to pass away from this world. He did not live to see his noble dream realized -- the dream of witnessing before his people the redemptive love of his Savior. However, there is a story of optimism behind it all; for his young manhood, like a grain of wheat, fell into the ground to die, and brought forth much fruit. Men and women, thereafter, who received the impact of his enriching spirit realized in no small degree a new impetus to missionary enterprise. Is there a meaning in the labors of those men and women who are giving their lives in far distant lands, where friends are few and opposition is great? What, after all, has Christianity done for the world? These are no easy questions to answer, but the richness that came into the life of the poor African boy after he had come in contact with the Christ furnished an apologetic that is most satisfying. Young men stood up in those eventful prayer meetings and declared their intention to go to Africa as missionaries. They threw away selfish ideals of life, accepted the challenge of the Cross, and not many years later left their homes and loved ones to share in the great task of helping build the Kingdom of God in the dark land of Sammy's birth. In the fall of 1893 Taylor University was moved to Upland, Indiana. The heavy indebtedness of the school at Fort Wayne, and the proposition of some Upland citizens to furnish the grounds and ten thousand dollars as a bonus to secure the college in

Upland, impelled the school authorities to make the transfer. However, the transfer did not, in the first year, prove very promising. The nation-wide panic which ensued the following year brought the institution to the brink of bankruptcy. The crisis became acute when in the dead of winter the lack of coal and other necessities brought such disappointment to the students that many threatened to leave school. Some of the professors had not received their salary for months. Many who claimed to be her supporters became discouraged, and ceased to help, thinking that Taylor's days were numbered and her future utterly hopeless.

But the year was saved through the heroic efforts of the faculty and some of the students. To them Taylor's difficulties did not furnish cause for yielding the struggle. They believed in the mission of the school and had faith that God's hand was upon it. Doctor Thaddeus Reade, its president, in the midst of that crucial period, was moved to write a brief sketch of the life of Sammy Morris, a little pamphlet that reached a total circulation of two hundred thousand copies. How much influence it had for the school in those terrible years of its history very few have ever realized. Doctor Burt W. Ayres now vice-president of Taylor University, whose official relation with the school dates back to 1897, has this to say about the part that Sammy indirectly played in the future of the school: "In the early years of my connection with Taylor University I was impressed with the wonderful influence of the life of Sammy Morris. Each fall many of the new students giving their religious experiences would speak of having read the booklet on the life of Sammy Morris written by President Reade, and tell how it was through that they had been influenced to come to Taylor. They spoke of the great blessing received from reading this brief account of his life. In those days gifts to the school were usually not in what we call large sums, but many who sent in money were moved to do so by the story of this wonderful life. The booklet was translated into a number of other languages in European countries and bore fruit, both material and spiritual. I distinctly remember checks as large as fifty and one hundred dollars -- very large gifts in those days -- coming from people in Norway, and Sweden. Not only did this little book bring students and gifts of money, but the large sale of the book brought in considerable money which was used to help educate worthy students who had no money and could not have remained in school but for these gifts and the employment given them by the school. Formerly, ministers would order these little books by the hundred and distribute them free, or sell them to their people when preparing for a revival, and they frequently wrote to the school telling of the wonderful spiritual uplift received.

"Many factors have entered into the life of Taylor University without anyone of which, humanly speaking, the school must have failed in the crucial decade just following the moving of the school to Upland. I believe the very life of the school depended upon the dynamic of this Spirit-filled life, preserved and released to the reading religious world by the pen of President Thaddeus C. Reade."

Hence, it was that little sketch with its triumphant message of love and faith that actually brought Taylor University before the eyes of Christian people, and drew students of spiritual aspirations from different states and countries to Taylor for their education. They were not misled. It is true the school was materially poor; the campus was not then so inviting as now; the buildings were not so attractive as the buildings of contemporary colleges, but the note of spirituality which dominated its student life, and the atmosphere of fellowship that characterized its classrooms and dormitories was something that to them was far more significant than Ionic pillars and Roman arches.

The coming of Sammy Morris to Taylor University also gave an idea as to the solution of the student-aid problem. It is to be understood that one of the dominant motives in the founding of Taylor University was that it might serve as a school where young people of limited means might secure an education. Doctor Reade's account of how this fund started is interesting: "A few weeks after Sammy came among us I was preaching in the village of Churubusco, in northern Indiana, and after a sermon I gave a brief account of our African boy and said as there was no fund provided for his support

we had taken him by faith. At the close
of the sermon a Brother Thomas slipped
a half dollar into my hand, and the next
morning as I was on my way to the train,
a Brother Kichler called me into his shop
and handing me a five dollar bill, said:
"The Spirit tells me to give this to your
faith fund." 'Faith fund!' This was a new
name, but we adopted it at once and this
proved to be the beginning of a fund
which has already helped more than two
hundred different students in their struggle
to secure an education, and it shall yet
help hundreds more. It is now five years
since Josiah Kichler gave that five dollar
bill to start the faith fund, but that fund
still lives. It has never been exhausted. It
has never at any time had fifty dollars to
its credit, for the contributions by which it
has been fed have been small, and as soon
as received were placed to the credit of
some indigent student, but there has been
-- Glory to God! -- there has always been

a "little oil in the cruse and a little meal in the barrel." The contributions to this faith fund have come to us by mail in amounts varying from one dollar to one hundred dollars. And from every state in the Union and from Canada. We have received two gifts of one hundred dollars each: one from the state of New Jersey, and one from far-off Sweden."

When Sammy died, all that belonged to his name, materially speaking, was the meager sum of eight dollars, an insignificant amount to start an endowment fund. But the life he lived and the spirit he left behind, are an inheritance of more value than any material legacy could have been. His brief biography, which reached a sale of two hundred thousand copies, at ten cents each, has given Taylor University twenty thousand dollars. Paradoxical, that a youth from the "Dark Continent," who left his homeland without a cent in his pocket, and whose maintenance at Fort Wayne was carried only on the principle of faith and charity, could bless hundreds of struggling students in their college education. But such is one of the achievements of Sammy's life and faith. There are men and women now in the great field of Christian service who should verily with bared heads pay homage to his memory; for without the faith fund of Taylor University it is doubtful if they could have attained their present position of leadership and responsibility. Indirectly, then, the young African has blessed the Christian work both in America and abroad by helping supply the needs of deeply consecrated men and women -- the greatest demands in the ministry of the Gospel.

But the pamphlet did more than that. Its phenomenal sale was not confined alone to America. It has been translated into different European languages, and into

Indian dialects, making it almost universal in its influence. Thus it brought Taylor University before the eyes of the world. It is not strange that gifts came from as far as Sweden, and many foreign students turned their attention to Upland, Indiana for their American education. The institution was then passing through her hard and trying days, but the publicity that went with the life of the Spirit-filled Kroo boy gave no little help in making the world know that somewhere there is a college that is great enough to care for the soul. One tribute the school has paid to the memory of that heroic character is the naming of Samuel Morris Hall, the dormitory that since 1908 has furnished many young men with a home. And here again is another instance of something strange. Who can imagine a college dormitory named after a poor, uncultured African youth! A proud civilization would strike a note of discord with such an act, but that only shows the spirit that dominates Taylor University. The college authorities, who saw fit to confer such an honor on the memory of the Kroo boy, were actuated by nothing less than the challenge of the principle to "render unto Caesar the things that are Caesar's and to God the things that are God's."

The building stands today. Hundreds of young men, many of them now holding responsible positions, have lived beneath its roof and their cultivated friendship and fellowships that have been among the deepest passions of their lives. Samuel Morris Hall! These are magic words that catch fire in the soul of many Taylor Alumni. And wherever those words were spoken they carried with them vivid rec- ollections of a life that voiced the trium- phant note of faith and love.

But the faith fund is not Sammy's greatest legacy to the school. He is immortalized in the hearts of the Taylor alumni, but not

because of the twenty thousand dollars
that he caused to go to Taylor University.
He aroused the missionary enthusiasm of
students and furthered the world vision
of the college, yet these are secondary to
that spiritual contribution which defined,
once for all, the position that Taylor was to
hold in the modern world. It is here that
he figured most largely in the history of
the institution: He perpetuated the spirit
of devotion and magnified the spiritual
aspirations of the student body. His simple
faith and loyalty to the vision of his soul
profoundly impressed those whom he met
and befriended, and gave them an acquaintance with his loving personality that
meant an acquaintance with the enduring realities of life. Back of all his sincere
prayers, back of all his ringing testimonies,
back of the inspiring expression upon his
spirit illuminated countenance, there was
the evident assurance that Sammy Morris
had laid hold richly upon the spirit which

actuated his Divine Master who came to bring life to a dying world. These thoughts quickened the minds of his friends and readers of his biography so that they were moved to search for themselves the way out of the seeming perplexities of life.

In other words, he showed Taylor University the value of a life that is totally surrendered to a father-like God. His never-dying spirit that prevails to this hour is a living witness to the truth that there is something real, something eternal in the things that cannot be seen nor heard. His glowing spiritual experiences emphasize the philosophy that "man cannot live by bread alone but by every word that cometh from the mouth of God." More than that, his faith is a testimony that somewhere, somehow, a tempest-tossed soul can find anchor within the haven of everlasting arms. Sammy was certain of his moorings. He could not fathom it, but in the fullness of his experience, he found that "love that will not let men go." He knew "in whom he had believed." He was sure that he had "a house not made with hands."

Taylor University is his monument; and her life, while true to academic and educational responsibilities, has never allowed itself to become indifferent to the deepest longings of the human soul. Her atmosphere, charged with the electric currents of intelligent spirituality, has influenced her students to revere the things that pertain to God; and hundreds of her graduates who are now in the open area of life, loyal to the visions that they caught at Taylor, have influenced thousands upon thousands of men and women to interpret the significance of the needs of their souls. Hence, the spirit and life of Sammy Morris is like the stone which when cast into the sea produces ripples that roll farther and farther until they reach the more distant shore.

This chapter is not complete if Sammy's relation to Doctor Thaddeus C. Reade is not discussed. It must be borne in mind that Sammy's influence could never have been felt outside of Taylor University if this "benefactor of struggling youths" had not written that brief sketch. Sammy lived the life, but it took a man of Doctor Thaddeus C. Reade's insight to interpret such a life.

One might ask how so poor and so homely a young man as Sammy could captivate the love and sympathy of a college president. But Doctor Thaddeus C. Reade saw in the African youth something real, something positive, which, if released to the world might help thousands to discover the infinite meaning of human life. He loved Sammy as his own son, and when death had seized the promising African youth, he wept and sobbed like a little child. "I

learned to love him as an own [sic] child
and from him I learned lessons of faith
and consecration to which I had been
an utter stranger before." The following
paragraph in his brief sketch of the life
of Sammy Morris reveals his affection
for the Kroo boy: "In writing this little
sketch, my only desire is that the people
may know what wonders our God can do
when he finds a willing, obedient, confid-
ing subject through whom and in whom
to work. Most of us, I fear, have gone too
far away from the simple faith of childhood, and God cannot do mighty works
in us because of our unbelief. The faith of
Sammy Morris never wavered and never
questioned; hence God, who chooses the
weak things to confound the mighty, put
His power upon him. I suppose that Mary
of Bethany never dreamed of acquiring
an immortal name; she scarcely knew the
meaning of such a thing. Her only ambi-
tion was to be known and loved by a little

circle of friends about her humble home, and to enjoy the approval of the Master who came and called on her. But because Mary anointed the feet of Jesus with costly nard and bathed them with her grateful tears and wiped them with her hair, her name was made immortal. 'Verily, I say unto you, wheresoever this gospel shall be preached, in the whole world, that also which this woman hath done, shall be spoken of as a memorial of her.' She probably had not the faintest idea of the far-reaching meaning of His words, but they teach us to honor all good works and perpetuate every noble example. If the subject of this sketch were alive and should be made acquainted with my purpose to publish to the world the simple story of his life, he would stare in blank amazement at the announcement. He would turn his honest, black face to mine, and after a few moments of thoughtful silence, he would slowly shake his head, and, raising his great eyes upward, he would say: "No, no, Mr. Reade; tell them not about poor Sammy Morris, but about Jesus. Tell them about the Holy Ghost." … To me this simple black boy was a daily wonder, a visible miracle of the utmost grace of God … I trust that in the story of his life he may prove a blessing to thousands of others as he has been to me and hundreds of others while living."

Samuel Morris and Thaddeus C. Reade; these are inseparable names. Where one is mentioned, the other must be. Both gave Taylor University gifts that can never die.

CHAPTER VI
What Can We Profit?

There are elemental values in the spiritual experiences and the moral struggle of Sammy Morris that must be emphatically pointed out before this book finds its close. It is true that he was only a poor African youth whose colored skin and kinky hair would betray a seeming inferiority of culture and intellect; but if something good can come out of Nazareth, then in this age, when men are beginning to see the peculiar contribution of every race and people to the common storehouse of world civilization, the Spirit-filled life of this colored youth has its place. Sammy Morris broke the alabaster box and anointed the feet of his Master with the sweet perfume of his simple faith. As a result, a memorial of enduring love and affection has been the tribute of thousands who glory in the things of the Spirit. He

belonged to a despised race, but in the
God of love in whose Kingdom human
personality is supreme, Sammy discovered
his appointed mission. His life was a fulfill-
ment of this mission; his death an interpretation of this sacred trust.

Sammy Morris lived, first of all, to bear a
triumphant testimony to the redemptive
power of the Christian religion. His life is
a challenge to those who deny the realities
of Calvary and the meaning of the Cross.
It is a proof of the fact that when the Jesus
of history becomes the Christ of one's
experience, something definite, something
wonderful enters into the personality of
everyone to make him a new creature
with new ideals and new aspirations. It is
a witness that "Jesus Christ is the world's
Redeemer on whom men of whatever race
and nationality can lay hold and realize
the great, ever living Spirit, the supreme
life that is through all and in all -- God." It

is a personal message that man's discovery
of God in Jesus Christ means the discovery of the way from darkness into light,
the loosening and falling of the crushing burdens from the bruised and aching
shoulders of mankind.

The miraculous change that took place
in his life, a change that has happened
in thousands of other lives that have embraced Jesus Christ as their Master, affords
Christianity the most effective apologetic.
Christianity is at the cross-roads. Minds
today, both of Asia and in the western
lands, are beginning to see that origins
and authority do not prove the certainty
of a religion. Mere proclamation of the
message is not sufficient. Can it help men
to a richer and fuller life? Can it transform
social life upon the earth into a kingdom
of righteousness? Its fruit, this is the test
that is being applied everywhere. Sammy
Morris -- an African son of the jungle,

of semi-savage parents, his childhood dwarfed by a heathen environment, a typical example of a broken personality -- surrendered his life to Jesus Christ, and behold, his soul so glowed with the richness and fullness of love and grace that those who met and saw him were moved to seek for themselves a more sublime interpretation of life. Here is something irresistible. When one sees such transformation that no science nor philosophy nor education can bring about, the world cannot help but be credulous to Christianity and sympathetic to the cause of Christian Missions.

Sammy Morris, secondly, in his contact with the American people during his brief sojourn in this country, is an expression of the best and highest that Christian Missions can do in the great program of mutuality and sharing. Here is a colored boy fresh from the jungles of Africa! Not one in a hundred would think that Christians [sic] Americans would owe to him lasting influences of spiritual power upon their lives. There are missionaries in the far corners of the world, not only for the reason that the redemptive love of God in Jesus Christ is a message that all men must hear, but also for the reason that Christianity embodies within itself that ideal of bringing the unique contributions of every people into a common storehouse where there is found "a positive and constructive effort to share the springs of spiritual power -- characterized by mutuality -- that attitude of mind in which passionate affection for and devotion to the values associated with one's own groups -- are combined with a sympathetic appreciation of values in all other groups."

Miss Knolls discovered Sammy Morris. She infused into him the richest and sublimest qualities of her soul. The colored boy opened his life to her and when the deepest in him had been touched, he sailed for America knowing not that his sojourn in this country was to contribute to the deepening spiritual life of the people who are sharing with the world their highest social and political achievements. In this act, the world finds a lesson: Discharge your spiritual energy to people of other culture and training so as to evoke from them the finest spiritual energy, for that in turn will come back to your own enrichment an eternal reciprocity among you who differ.

Again the life of Sammy Morris is rich in the guiding principle that may well serve as one of the bases for bringing different races and nationalities into a common understanding. Much of the present wrangling between white and colored people is due to the fact that one has been accustomed to look at the other simply from the human standpoint. It is hard to regard with friendly attitude those whom one is accustomed to dislike and look down upon. But strange indeed, Sammy Morris, in his contact with the American people made his friends, hearers, and readers of his biography forget that he belonged to a despised race. He broke the prejudices and dislikes of the people with whom he came in contact because he brought in with that contact -- God. He did not force men and women to like him. He showed them that God loved him. His personality was an invitation to cooperate with God's purpose for him. His was a life that made men feel that ethical living is not concerned with what one can find in man, but what can possibly be created in that man. He was an appeal to love men not as they are but to love the man in men, the man who is the object of God's interest and love, the man for whom Christ died. "I felt that he was of God" is the common utterance of those who saw and knew him. In his personality Christianity varied a message that humanity as a whole has a common unity in its possession of the intrinsic worth of the human soul in every individual, be he a member of the yellow, black, brown, or white race.

Sammy Morris' faith, furthermore is a testimony that the reality of Christian religion consists not in the grandeur of its rights and ceremonies, nor in the theories of God's goodness and ideas of His mercy, but in His living love that flowed into man's heart. Sammy knew that "He is, and that He is a rewarder of them that diligently seek him." In his spiritual life, in the deep and secret exercise of his soul's highest power, in his life of faith and hope and love and prayers, he met and touched the living God. No mere vision of a fetish-ridden mind caused the strange and loud shouts in the lonely hours of the night in the coffee plantation of Liberia. His visions were real -- the contact of his spirit with the Divine, the wrestling of his soul with God so certain and so lasting that they left marks upon his body and mind forever. Yes, God came to him and laid hold upon him. In the quiet of Liberian jungles, on the angry waves of the rough Atlantic, in the packed congregation of worshippers, in the solitude of his room, he felt a vital consciousness of God. To him, it was He who delivered his soul in great temptation, and in the midst of anguish forgave his sins and dried the tears from his eyes in the hours of his bitter sufferings. God to him was real -- God pardoned his sins, upheld his spirit, comforted him in grief, and lifted the star of his hope. He was the one in whom he lived and had his being -- the living and true God that is in Jesus Christ.

Sammy Morris, lastly, lived to remind men

everywhere that the glory of life does not consist simply in the things that can be seen by the eyes nor heard by the ears, nor in the abundance of the things one possesses. Life is more than raiment; it is more than the senses; it is more than the quest for daily bread; man is a spirit, hence he must be fed with things of the spirit.

Moreover, these things that can be touched, weighed, and perceived are transitory, and then in the long run they do not constitute the final values of life. Man is so careful and troubled about many things. But one thing is needful, and Sammy had chosen that good part which shall not be taken from him. His soul lived and trusted in God. God was his refuge and strength, a very present help in trouble. While some trust in chariots, and others in houses, he remembered the name of the Lord. Hence all who had seen him recognized in him an irresistible personality. It beamed in his face; it looked out of his eyes; it spoke in his voice; it showed in his action. Doubts, pain, suffering, sickness, death -- he triumphed over them. His spirit was unconquerable.

This power of his spirit, this strength of his faith in the mastery of circumstance, can all be traced back to those hours of struggle and toil when he tarried alone in the "Wilderness" of his room. He spent more than forty days of his Christian life in fasting and praying. He paid greater heed to the thirst of his inner life, and consequently he found the key that unlocks the meaning of life. It was spiritual insight born of inward and hidden contact with God.

Sammy Morris! This is his last message: "In our very laudable enthusiasm over action and social morality and class equality and hygienic conditions and international policies and tangible results, we

are beginning to forget the inner life of
the soul, the quiet turning of the spirit
back upon itself, which in the rhythmic
life of man is quite as important as is the
outward-going impulse. In our safe and
sane and sober fear of emotionalism and
sentimentality, we seem tempted to disown
the spiritual nature which is part of our
human heritage. The glow of feeling, the
sense of the Infinite, the intuition of the
Beyond, the aspiration for the more than
earthly, these are and always must be an
important, if not an essential, part of religion. And they are genuinely human as
well -- as genuinely natural ends as are the
biological processes of digestion, assimila-
tion, and reproduction. It is certainly of
great importance that we should consider
what we and our slum friend shall eat, and
what we shall drink and wherewithal we
shall be clothed; but there are one or two
things which are well to seek, and perhaps
the 'Kingdom of God' consists just in the

physical and social conditions. I cannot forget that one who spoke with some authority on this matter said, 'The Kingdom of God is within you.'

"In short every age has need of 'the contemplative life,' and ours is no exception to the rule. It might, in fact, be maintained that our twentieth century stands in special need of it. When, indeed, could its importance be more properly emphasized than at a time when Activity is the shibboleth of theory and Efficiency the matter of practice; when we are brought up to feel that at every moment we must be working or else we must be amused, and taught to believe that most real values are to be appraised in terms of economic productivity? Even social justice, and college settlements, and industrial democracy and international amity are not enough to satisfy the full warm life of the soul. The soul needs a larger draft of air, a less circumscribed horizon than even these excellent things can give. It needs a chance for spreading its wings, for looking beyond itself, beyond the immediate environment, and for quiet and inner growth, which is best to be found in that group of somewhat indefinite but very real experiences -- aspiration, insight, contemplation -- which may well be called the mystic life."*

*   *   *   *

In the fall of 1927 the members of the Senior Class of Taylor University visited the grave of Sammy Morris at a Ft. Wayne cemetery. The humble little tombstone that was almost buried among autumn's leaves was so touching a scene that on their return to the campus they felt that he, who has meant so much to the development of Taylor University, and has thrilled thousands of souls with the beautiful message of his life, deserved a more enduring monument over his burial place.

THE OLD GRAVESTONE

THE ANGEL IN EBONY

The citizens of Fort Wayne, through the sponsorship of the 1928 Senior Class of Taylor University, enthusiastically rallied with their financial cooperation, so that today, across the stone bridge, some fifty yards from the old burial place, upon a hill that in spring and summer smiles with Nature's richest blossoms, a rugged but appropriate monument, expressive of his life and religion, now permanently stands. In the distance one catches this inscription:

Samuel Morris
1873-1893
Prince Kaboo
Native of West Africa

* * * *

Famous Christian Mystic
Apostle of Simple Faith
Exponent of the Spirit-filled life

* * * *

THE ANGEL IN EBONY

*Student at Taylor University 1892-3
Fort Wayne, now located at Upland, Ind. The
story of his life a vital contribution to the development of Taylor University.*

* * * *

*The erection of this memorial was sponsored by
the 1928 class Taylor University, and funds were
contributed by Fort Wayne citizens.*

*James Bisset Pratt's "The Religious Con-
sciousness" PP. 478, 479.

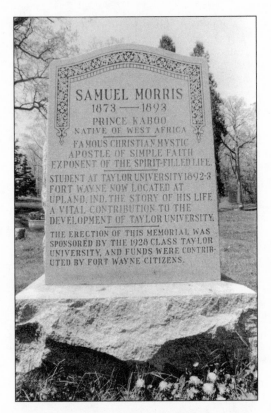

New Monument erected by Class of 1928
In Lindenwood Cemetery, Fort Wayne

APPENDIX

Sammy Morris left behind no written work of any kind. He would be unequal to such a task. The following sayings which have been preserved in Dr. Reade's pamphlet reveal Sammy's spiritual conception of life:

"Bread is one thing, stone is another. I once saw a stone with gold in it and they told me that it was worth more than a barrel of flour. But when I am hungry I cannot eat that stone, I must have bread. So my soul cannot be satisfied with anything but Jesus, the bread of life."

"Living a religious life is like eating meat. Some parts of the meat are lean and you like them very much. Some parts are fat and you do not like them at all. But you must eat both lean and fat to be healthy and strong. So religion has its joys and crosses; you love joys but you draw back from crosses. However, you must take both of them to become strong, healthy Christian."

The following hymns are his favorites. They are expressive of his mystical life. The first speaks of the soul's joy and satisfaction in its discovery of Jesus Christ as a Savior. The second utters a note of preparedness. It is interesting, however, to notice the frequent repetition of verses. It is very expressive of negro melody and the negro type of music. Sammy, when visiting the homes of his Fort Wayne friends, would ask that these hymns be sung as part of his entertainment.

Fade, Fade Each Earthly Joy

Fade, fade each earthly joy,
  Jesus is mine
Break every tender tie
  Jesus is mine!
Dark is the wilderness,

THE ANGEL IN EBONY

Earth has no resting place,
Jesus alone can bless,
  Jesus is mine!

Tempt not my soul away,
  Jesus is mine!
Here would I ever stay,
  Jesus is mine!

Perishing things of clay,
Born but for one brief day,
Pass from my heart away,
  Jesus is mine!

Farewell, ye dreams of night,
  Jesus is mine!
Lost in the dawning light,
  Jesus is mine!
All that my soul has tried
Left but a dismal void,
Jesus has satisfied,
  Jesus is mine.

Farewell, mortality,
  Jesus is mine!
Welcome eternity
  Jesus is mine!
Welcome, O love and blest
Welcome my Savior's breast
  Jesus is mine.

Behold the Bridegroom

Are you ready for the Bridegroom
  When he comes, when he comes?
Are you ready for the Bridegroom
  When he comes, when he comes?
Behold! he cometh! Behold, he cometh,
  Be rob'd and ready, for the Bridegroom
  comes.

Have your lamps trimm'd and burning
  When he comes, when he comes;
Have your lamps trimm'd and burning
  When he comes, when he comes;
He quickly cometh, He quickly cometh
  O soul be ready when the Bridegroom
  comes.

We will all go out to meet him
    When he comes, when he comes;
We will all go out to meet him
    When he comes, when he comes;
He surely cometh, he surely cometh
    We'll go out to meet him when the
    Bridegroom comes.

We will chant allelujias,
    When he comes, when he comes;
We will chant allelujias,
    When he comes, when he comes;
Lo! Now he cometh, Lo now he cometh!
    Sing allelujias, for the Bridegroom
    comes.

The 14th chapter of St. John, Sammy's
favorite chapter in the Bible, is very sug-
gestive of his Christian faith and life. On
Sunday evening when the students in
the dormitory would pay a visit to one
another, Sammy's guests were always re-
quested to read this chapter. Then prayer

would follow. It might be said here that he was not retiring as many would think he was. He took active part in the activities of the literary societies. An old alumnus of Fort Wayne Methodist College told the author that Sammy once sang an African song in the program of the Philalethean Literary Society.

There are five great messages in this chapter. It deals with Jesus' account of his coming for his own, of Jesus as one with the Father, of the new promise and privilege of prayer, of the promise of the Spirit, and of the bequest of peace, all touching the peaks of Christian hope, love and peace.

1. Let not your heart be troubled: ye believe in God, believe also in me.
2. In my Father's house are many mansions: if it were not so, I would have told you. I go to prepare a place for you.

3. And if I go and prepare a place for you, I will come again, and receive you unto myself; that where I am, there ye may be also.

4. And whither I go ye know, and the way ye know.

5. Thomas saith unto him, Lord, we know not whither thou goest; and how can we know the way?

6. Jesus saith unto him, I am the way, the truth, and the life: no man cometh unto the Father, but by me.

7. If ye had known me, ye should have known my Father also: and from henceforth ye know him, and have seen him.

8. Philip saith unto him, Lord, shew us the Father, and it sufficeth us.

9. Jesus saith unto him, Have I been so long time with you, and yet hast thou not known me, Philip? he that hath seen me hath seen the Father; and how sayest thou then, Shew us the Father?

10. Believest thou not that I am in the

Father, and the Father in me? The words that I speak unto you I speak not of myself: but the Father that dwelleth in me, he doeth the works.

11. Believe me that I am in the Father, and the Father in me: or else believe me for the very works' sake.

12. Verily, verily, I say unto you, He that believeth on me, the works that I do shall he do also; and greater works than these shall he do; because I go unto my Father.

13. And whatsoever ye shall ask in my name, that will I do, that the Father may be glorified in the Son.

14. If ye shall ask any thing in my name, I will do it.

15. If ye love me, keep my commandments.

16. And I will pray the Father, and he shall give you another Comforter, that he may abide with you forever;

17. Even the Spirit of truth; whom the world cannot receive, because it seeth him

not, neither knoweth him: but ye know him; for he dwelleth with you, and shall be in you.

18. I will not leave you comfortless: I will come to you.

19. Yet a little while, and the world seeth me no more; but ye see me: because I live, ye shall live also.

20. At that day ye shall know that I am in the Father, and ye in me, and I in you.

21. He that hath my commandments, and keepeth them, he it is that loveth me: and he that loveth me shall be loved of my Father, and I will love him, and will manifest myself to him.

22. Judas saith unto him, not Iscariot, Lord, how is it that thou wilt manifest thyself unto us, and not unto the world?

23. Jesus answered and said unto him, If a man love me, he will keep my words: and my Father will love him, and we will come unto him, and make our abode with him.

24. He that loveth me not keepeth not my sayings: and the word which ye hear is not mine, but the Father's which sent me.

25. These things have I spoken unto you, being yet present with you.

26. But the Comforter, which is the Holy Ghost, whom the Father will send in my name, he shall teach you all things, and bring all things to your remembrance, whatsoever I have said unto you.

27. Peace I leave with you, my peace I give unto you: not as the world giveth, give I unto you. Let not your heart be troubled, neither let it be afraid.

28. Ye have heard how I said unto you, I go away, and come again unto you. If ye loved me, ye would rejoice, because I said, I go unto the Father: for my Father is greater than I.

29. And now I have told you before it come to pass, ye might believe.

30. Hereafter I will not talk much with you: for the prince of this world cometh,

and hath nothing in me.

31. But that the world may know that I love the Father; and as the Father gave me commandment, even so I do. Arise, Let us go hence.

THE ANGEL IN EBONY